published 2019 by Northern
Undercurrents

ISBN 978-0-9958247-7-5

cover artwork by Janelle Hardy

For all the beautiful
strangers who've brought
gifts…

These two trees
wrapped by storm
have leaned on each other
and cut through bark
with the passing of days
and cold nights…

may they stretch
into their deep roots

so life flows more fully
in each

a separate flowering
of two species

still wrapped,

uniquely twisted

marked by time

two shapes

shaping.

Is there more?
or have the sweet moments
burned away
dew in the heat of day

these ornery words
caught in my throat

surely not just hormones
but wild wisdom
trying to rip her way out

scratching to freedom

never before
have I felt so sure
of my claws

ragged sheathing
no longer protects

the others withdraw
from my bristling

I could exult
except I'm just too mad.

Peace like a rock tumbler,
louder than expected

all this contact
grinding,

smoothing over time.

This active wave,
broad rush of calm
with turbulence,
organic bubbling

– may I stop craving
stillness,
the kind that fears movement.

You lovely waterball
sloshing
in vacuum

warmed gently
side to side

caressed by photons
that dance at your poles

all these constructions of mind
obscuring our love

distracting our deep knowing.

May we sink our noses
deep in your sage,
your roses,
pine, olive, jungle moss

surf slithering
to touch sand and ice floe,
rising
to fall fresh in our open mouths.

May we honour glinting eyes
that fly and gallop,
dig and dive.

May we feel the belly shame
of their departures,
how we have elbowed our way through
this creature crowd,
our destructive greed.

May we learn from expiration
the gifts of trees,

4

transforming our noxious imbalance
to necessary breath

sustainable collaboration,
resilient tending

a sacred belonging.

"No problem" even as problems brush my mind and try to provoke more tightening, fixing, admonishments. Softness… I want to offer more encouragement and recognition to others, soft kindness moving in flow, no need to "do" except that these invitations need uttering in some form, whether glance or touch or words. No need to push or prove anything, except as the softness itself feels called to move, to cavort, to invite outside to play in the world.

Of course that impulse gets wrapped in agendas and judgments and deadlines… but the urge to keep unwrapping, loosening, making room – this is what is most fiercely honourable, most in need of exposure and outward flooding.

Channels are created in the movement of this softness, etched into the clay of personality and soul and lifestyle, creating avenues of direction as the result of flow itself.

All these years
it's been humour
to my rescue

my anxious yelps
stopped
by how silly they sound

my tears
splashing over lips
that twitch,
propelled by irony.

It's not that I can't hear;
I feel pain
moved by stories

but when they push me
to a precipice,
a dark and stormy night

… there's Snoopy, typing.

My mother
wants to mother me;
oh yes the real one too,
but she who lives inside
is not just the mother to other…
she embraces,
or holds strong arms ready
to enfold on my return.
I forgot all this
in the giving,
heard her name
as duty,
felt her as a phase
I needed to live through.
What puzzling relief,
remembering Her fierce love,
unwavering pledge
to wholeness
including my own.

The taste
of impatience

like coffee
poured too soon
in the brewing

or wind
sounding sharp
through bare branches

no leaves
to soothe its passing

yet.

That you might feel
whatever temperature
of air on skin

perhaps on an ankle
or forearm

or pausing to notice
the difference.

That you might feel
that happy pain
in your middle

a breath
longing for more pull

and one more.

That your ears
might soften
to receive more than one
layer of sound

and hear the blend
as it passes.

Those chairs
that made me cry
are covered in snow

but we could sit today
with wet bums,
still breathing

and grin at the way

empty and full

are sudden
and decay

emptiness holding such shapes,
beloved.

I am choosing
exactly what I said

this birthday year
with surprising decisions

a decadence of will

and counter-will.

That ego is not happy
with my freedom,

muttering her threats

and I choose to hear her
with a grin,

not ignoring her dread

but frolicking anyway.

12

Small Town

Intertwinings,
these pleasures
cause pain

and also all the soothing,
building up strands of care

brave looking
at what is true
and hurts

brave rejoicing
at all the new beginnings.

Folding sheets

most people
enjoy fresh sheets
just sometimes

me with all these beds

folding every day

how the mind
makes drudgery
of privilege

how our litanies
of burden

can become the same words
new melodies

songs of joy.

I call upon
the people of the slump,
slouching,
sighing,
letting go
of creative fire.

May we
who can't get off the couch
hold soft

open former firmness

feel time move
without our help

nod weakly
to what is unmoving.

Dreadful predicament,
this waking each day
to all the ways
I wrap my arms
around my ribs

trying to offer comfort,
wailing belly
protesting.

O let me cradle
all these aches
in open arms

extend my reach
so light has room

travelling through
space and time

to touch planets
in near orbits
with their own
soft skins.

I am teetering on the edge of hopelessness – can hear the voices of despair, pointlessness, defeat – but choose to land my feet into a loving groundlessness, not "escape" but just opening my heart to my worries and my loves, my joys. Free-fall rather than cling. Show up with curiosity and love and fresh eyes over and over again.

While I've written these sentences, the sky has changed from grey to rose and blue. The planet keeps turning, so do my moods. May I keep listening, keep loving, keep finding healthy boundaries so my kindness can thrive.

In a world
that might end

sooner than expected

may I savour

how my heart leaps gladly
when the sunrise strokes magenta

how my lips part
at the scent of pine

how poplar buds
stay tucked inside
their shiny scales
until evenings lose their frost.

May I too drink up
from my feet

spring sap melting our days,

nurture future flowering,

protecting what is here.

If I keep waiting
for the day of safety

when I could walk
and know where my foot will land

or speak
and know approval

or smile,
guaranteed a smile in return

my walking
and speaking
and smiling

will never happen.

May I feel
the long tremble
called living

and let it wobble me
through the discomfort
of being here;

may I know the freedom
of causing necessary pain,
faithful to the healing.

That particular now
before they turned off the light

when I watched
its glimmering
like an invitation

brightness wavered
with the motion of water;
steady shining blurred
under constant ripples

making it flash
in my perception,
catching my eye
due to inconstancy

that blessed flow.

And me without a pen
or a plan
just felt surprised
when it disappeared

a withdrawn hand

a memory of welcome.

Sunlight on snow
was so powerful

not electricity
or lasers
but the realness
of travelled light
brightening

landing on water
in a state of fluff

clearing all obstacles
with the force of heat and cold,
illumination.

And so I lay down in it,
as did the dog,
his trembling
forceful

I had never noticed
his excitement
or fear
in quite this way

while blue sky
and patient bare branches
stretched for more noticing.

Heroine

I see
on this cold day

how my addiction
drops me

these wild vials

the dread scenes
I inject

compulsively
playing out pretend wins.

Saving the day
at a cost;

puncturing my now
with scary tomorrows

fear tracks
scarring my soft skin.

No longer hidden,
this habit
needs breaking,

encouraging friends.

Holes in walls,
wiring ripped away;
not a quiet vanishing,

an angry departure
and messy defiance.

Where there had been beauty,
just ugly scars,

where care and healing were thriving,
a dangerous wounding.

Whose rage? why secret?

Not vandalism,
a ruthless gathering
of precious particulars,

a tragic freedom,

a jarring vindication
at such cost.

Off kilter
they used to say

and as I practice,

looking to ride
this different axis

for the sake of my spine
and so much more

may I trust
the gravity
in my own orbit

magnetic strength
journeying
around the sun.

My pen keeps twitching to write about this or that occurrence, this or that sensation or concern… and while I open to more sensitivity, more consciousness and paying attention, I also need the counterbalance of more ease, more spacious relaxing, more surrender to flow and not-holding.

I can trust that I will know or remember what I need to, but that most of my experience will evaporate each day like the rainbow in a soap bubble, precious and gone.

Appreciate deeply but do not grip or own or hang on. Love each moment for itself only. I will play with more freedom from story… experiment with dropping my desire for coherence, for stories that make sense… live more like a kaleidoscope, shifting moments of meaningless colour and light.

Hysteria

The reason we know
lobotomies
were not a good idea

is because women
never bothered with them.

If the knitting circle
had noticed a good use for them

how much kindness…

when Sadie cried
with midlife despair

dear Agnes and Betsy
would have shared a look,
and Delores cleared space
on the kitchen table

all of them waiting
for Georgina's special crochet hook

a timely solution
for Sadie's pain,
a wise relief,
supported.

Why write a poem
when I want to draw a map

compose instructions
to get me from here
to where I might want to go

if I knew where that was?

Something more practical,
more useful,
than ink on page

or breathing with attention;

I'd skip the exhales
if I could,
impatient.

The shape of my body
could be happier;
I don't even know
if this means
more or fewer
indulgences.

I see too in my sisters
how the tides
of pain and pleasure
shape their shores,
how receding
and extending
are in steady rhythm,
how the clothes that used to fit
grow saggy or pinched,
how the optimal state
is only a size
we pass through occasionally.

May we find comfort
in ribs or rolls,
and wear that comfort
freely,

knowing the shapes
are in flux,

take refuge
in whatever body
we are wearing,
tasting life.

For a long time
I've judged
my baby steps

imagining long strides
and greater distance

a fantasy
of confident moves.

Today
with the pace of bulging twigs
I can drop delusion

forget both ice and leaves

feel my natural now

wobble and wonder
sustaining my frame.

I'm grateful for every tree planted, even in thoughtless monoculture, for the oxygen it brings to our planetary lungs.

May we keep encouraging our wiser voices, our complex wisdoms, our practices of diversity and sustainability instead of our urgent fixing that creates new shortcomings.

I tend to frame this as feminist, taking the wider view, the longer and deeper connections, the more eloquent and patient commitments to not causing harm. But it's really not about women and men, it's about listening to the deeper rhythms of a gender-rich life force, a planet wisdom that wants all species to thrive, that wants the wise ones among us to curtail the shortsighted greed of powerfully adolescent systems.

These fragile words,
just petals
lightly expressing
the tips
of what is tree

brief soft beauties
tossed in breeze

participating
in the nurturing

fecundity, surrender

and so tiny
in relation to trunk
roots
rivers of fluids and microbes

underground webs of forest

slow rich geysers
powerful explosions unseen

these deep risings,

such delicate incarnation.

Today the palm tree is still
in the way life is
small ripples
in constant motion
each frond
responding to air

even the breath of birds
released in calling
stirs currents.

Yesterday
it taught me of tenacity,
trunk rooted
while breeze whipped frantic dancing

today at first glance
so quiet.

Every year
we glue his head back on;

adhesive holds
through Christmas

but something dries out
while he lies in a box.

My head too
wobbles

I need the glow
of lights on spruce

intentional remembering
of love

help to recover
alignment

liquid kindness
patching.

I really need to keep softening into kindness for myself, with the genuine aspiration that this kindness will spill out to others. Which is energetically very different from trying to find reserves of kindness inside me, sacrificing my own energy.

When I'm kind to myself first, I'm letting love flow, letting it be here… melting the sense of "me" and "other" by relaxing into love.

Then love itself gets to flow where it wants to go, where it will be absorbed or flow over, like water in a stream that can move through tiny gills or over rocks but does not make a condition of being received.

Where is the yes?

Why is my throat
so choked

this quiet
inarticulate

how have I lost propulsion
for such a short word?

Just air and muscles
are needed

and I have both

but the daughter of the wild

is bruised and aching,

her voice in her belly

lacks momentum

for even the short distance
to an open mouth.

Calliope I

That awkward celebration,
a wild huffing

music pitched
by rustic tents

a carnival
of simple invitations

to dance
and laugh
at these small wonders

a grand design
reduced
to these fatigued farmers

beautiful respite
weathered hands clapping

like a train whistle
pointing to a journey

simple melodies
close to home.

Calliope II

Your name
a bell in darkness

muse of ages
touching lips with fire

sweet elegant ache

a red cord
through all of us

a reverence so profound
that even bitter jokes
pay homage

your wild music
our own

your joy
as tears or laughter

your truth splashing.

Ingratitude
the taking

the blindness to living

that curbs my foot,

blinkers on my eyes

stepping on all precious green.

And not just me

but all of us

and the despair of it

and too the whiffs
like mint or parsley
underfoot

compelling my soft descent
tenderly reaching for ground.

May I love me
so fully
that it's ok
when others don't.

May I stop
the constant angling
for love

put down my rod and net

feel the water
instead of seeking fish

feel the water on my toes
as deep immersion
in plenty

know that my heart
can drink always

replenishing
an endless generosity.

Divine kindness,
may I coax
the fist
in my belly
to be an open palm

rest
in the awkward pulsing

vibrate
in the deepest strands,
embodied soul.

And then,
from my wild and shaking heart,
receive the tender pain
of those who call me forward

crumpled on a journey
or lost in fog

my heart
washing their wounds
in the largest bath of all,

sending out the sweetest joy

glimpsing their play.

Mother "the other." Embrace, welcome, get bigger. Love beyond what is rational. Get past yourself. Care deeply. Get curious. Grow your welcome. Acknowledge kinship everywhere. Unleash body wisdom. Tend your trees. Tend your own body. Tend other bodies. Smile at your foes. Nurture goodness. Recognize pain, speak truth. Melt walls. Open borders. Create supple, healthy boundaries. Water gardens. Plant wisely. Collaborate courageously. Ask brave questions. Tremble with generosity. Generate fierce kindness. Clean up a shoreline.

Not like air traffic
controlling planes in flight

although I know
that intensity

now I aspire
to lean back
on a rough tree

stretch my neck
gently

observing one flight
if it appears

in this one frame,
my visible sky.

Even with terror
in my body
or this steady low-level fear

may kindness
be the fuel
pumping my mouth and hands.

My body
this intricate array
chemicals
and shared parasites,
sinews and sensations,
electricity
in emotions and scents

…rich data
and me a luddite,
fumbling at switches

habits of poking
delicate instruments

navigating blind

to the health of me.

This tender gut,
not metaphor,
painful belly button

pressed

like a buzzer
with electric shock

who knew
I had such a frazzled nerve

receptacle of refuse
for decades

waiting for a day,
a siamese fatigue and curiosity

probing fingers
igniting old yelps

staying with deep indignities

hoping the breathless vulnerable

releases space for more.

I welcome happiness;

sounds obvious

but o what a journey

bouldering my aversions
shouldering all these burdens

turning aside
from all the warm springs

no good reason.

Now at the plateau
distinct from any peak

broad view
invites this naked wind

neither warm nor cool;

I drop all pretense

and feel it.

There was a woman
who thought she knew things

and found they changed
like slippery tadpoles

into louder croakings

different than expected,
not sleek.

And these frogs
leapt over each other
eating flies
and grunting;

some memory
of swimming more smoothly

causing a pause

and in the dark night
their warbles
sounded like song.

I notice how my clarity and momentum get "foggy" very quickly these days. I'm trying to be aware and motivated and indeed many of the things I experienced as "obstacles" are quietly coming into focus, finding resolution.

I'm "untraining" or "re-wiring" my habits of crisis and worry and too much anticipating. I'm consciously bringing lots of gratitude into each day and I'm aware that I get to experience more beauty and sweetness than many people.

May I keep "waking up" with vitality and love; continuing to rest and care for my body but not sleepwalking through my days. Movement and connection.

May I keep learning how to welcome "what arises" as energy that nurtures my living rather than depletes it. It's an important perspective, a game-changer for the way I want to live.

Distilling syllables,
fermenting sweet arisings

filtering through this complex web
called me

the muck of days
made potent
with time

risking explosion
and waste

may I have patience
in my caring

alert trust
in the slow drip,
melody of flavours absorbing

refined end notes
only possible
by waiting

tending slowness.

Inukshuk

The path was not easy
and I got lost more than once

saw you standing
with your profile against the sky

cold beauty
and fallen rocks.

I thought to linger,
caress your stones

but that weighted chill
was pointing

and soon not just my gaze
but also my toes
went in a new direction

seeking home.

Sweet seeing
this recognition
we can call love

a deep bowing

a scampering of grin

beloved neighbour

subway smile

scolding squirrel

...invitations to wake,

stretch,

pores and perceptions

open.

Tired joy,
maybe that's the best kind

too fatigued
to shine

collapsed in a bright puddle
softness pooled

a worn affection
with holes

comforting love.

The monkey on my back
slid around to my front

like a toddler monster
clutching my whole torso

black gripping
clinging to my neck
squishing my heart

pinning my solar plexus
so that I can't expand

little legs encircling my belly
tail a fierce diaper
blocking my flow.

Addicted to my ego
we stumble through this home

me off balance and staggering.

I choose to ask for help
to peel off this wild burden,

let my lover
and my friends
see what lives beneath.

A clock
needing lubrication

a ticking of bones,
the sound of time
not spent in flow

may these reminders
nudge my moving

awaken me
to the finite

even as I remember
that clocks
are humble servants
in time's household.

I'd like my innocence back,
happy illusions
of improvement

life filled with smiles
and reasons to cheer

when goals
felt like pathways

when love
seemed it would always
say yes

when the children
had clear eyes
intensely curious

when I knew
how to play.

May this longing
turn my body now,
slipping free from
yesterday or tomorrow,
shaping movements
in these currents of air.

When I dance
fully immersed

the folds of time's dress
swirl around me

touching with love

my past and future selves,

silk caressing faces
that spring from my heart,

loved ones spinning in the sky
and breathing now.

My arms invoke
a fiery peace,
ambrosia of courage
to warm the belly

an ointment of repairing

an unction of injunction

a beautiful mending.

These beloved names
are making me
so tense

causing me to twist
in fear
around this anxious belly.

I can imagine
freedom
a sea of kindness

but imagination
pulls me out of now;

the stretch required
in every breath

lungs
massaging my innards
when I let them move.

A random conversation with my
neighbour… so little is actually random,
more like little beads collecting side by
side to make flowers and patterns we
can't see until they grow.

But just last night, two women at 50
talking about our hormones, our
menstruation and the surges of heat
that have arrived like strangers
expected on the road.

I'm amazed by the capacities of
women, the way we can dip into
intimate conversation without shame,
how we can welcome true stories like
deer drinking water, smelling for
freshness and licking up what's offered.
And moving on. I may never have
another talk with her like that again,
and it's ok. Or as neighbours we may
interconnect into our 80s.

I'm enjoying this season of stirrings, of
feeling seeds crack open underground,
no visible growth on the surface but a
deep ovulation in the soil of my days.

My fear
keeps standing
in the canoe

trying to take charge
at the stern

rocking my ride

through these rapids.

May I keep finding invitation
so she kneels

muttering

contributing her strength

while I steer
the best I can

and pay attention
to the river.

Moving forward,
for too long
I shrugged things off
or pretended I was immune
to arrows

or soldiered on
in full armour

or let shame stop me
in my tracks.

Moving forward,
I want to sway
by choice,

laugh a little
at my lurching,

stumble with dignity
and a soft heart

trying less hard,
trusting my friendship with me
is big enough for others.

That current
sparks live

I turn away
and
turn towards
this powerful discomfort

not just fear
but excitement

knowing nothing
in so many shapes

and though there is work
in listening
to all these versions of me

may I keep moving

provoked by the buzz,

source-propelled.

Bells in the night,

I hear phone calls
invisible on my phone,

summons

to rise sharply

to sit with a free pen
scratching before dawn.

Relevance

unmasked as common fraud

not common good, but gain

hiding a desire to be liked.

May happiness break free
from its grip,

may the tongue tasting bitter in us all

find peace.

To be the kind of person
who pauses for tea

not ritual

responding to the knock,
the woman framed
by light and cold

who wants to wrap her hands
on something warm

and share her tears
or silence.

Like a planetwalker
with a small trajectory

may I still the rushing,
heat water,
maintain an empty table

and an unlocked door.

Pain
like aged whiskey

valuable and burning

smoothed by patient attention
over years

dangerously potent.

An expensive gift,

high costs

residual risks

requiring mastery,
true crafting.

May we sip gently,
welcome the taste
of this bitter warmth

notice the joy
in its astringent flavour

mellowing.

These arms
have held
many beautiful moments

people who gave
and received
and bathed me in love

bags of groceries
and buckets of earth

firewood, huge boxes

… and now
they hang limp

getting ready
to embrace

my terror,

befriend my dread.

My belly-borne
are returning

lovely feathers bent

and I've been afraid
of this nest

the wobbly tree
it's perched on,
the wind.

The size of them
and how nothing is cozy,
how they don't fit
under my wings.

My terror
in watching them
fly by falling.

And oh how beautiful
the shimmering,
light on each curved wing

learning to fight air
and yield,
pennaceous;

colours of hair and eye
known to me so deeply
in different shades of day

rupturing my heart
past my scarcity of nest

tearful joy
in a blowing sky.

Have had some beautifully inspiring moments and encounters the past few days, as well as these counterpoints of pain, anxiety, the "blah" recognitions, the boring self-inventories.

No easy reconciliation between these extremes of exquisite perception and the everyday whining that arises. My friend is struggling these days with the loss of excitement, how her season feels flat and full of ennui. I keep encouraging her to accept the boredom, stop trying to escape it but just accept that it will change.

I'd like to pretend that the moments when I glow will just keep getting stronger and more radiant. But the truth is that I'm stronger when I can embrace my own blah with the same patience that I embrace the wow.

Pursuing some ideal of constant wow actually sucks me out of the vitality of real living.

I just saw
for a flash

less than a minute
of wisdom

but I'll take what I can get.

The ways I've been trying to remodel,
pick open my nest
to make more room
for others to roost

sort out room
for me
in the jostling

be nice
in the ways I show love
in the crowding.

May I trust instead
that there is shelter
wherever I fly,

may I teach
by my actions

plummet and soar

in full view.

As a fever
breaks

skin unexpectedly
cooled

or a river
frozen for months

cracks under pressure
and flows

ice
just a memory

so may love
wend its way
through our twisted bodies

soften our rigid poses

splitting our pain

like a bread loaf crumbled,

morsels to feed others.

My little world
with its tight protests
against a full breath

and squints
against headaches
and various cramps

expands sometimes,
attending to needs,
welcoming

a busy list
with legs.

So when my little world
can feel its own axis,
some deep magnetic tilt

there is such wonder
instantly

a kinship with trees,
genetic heritage with fish,
miracles of gravity
suspending us just so

between the tugs of suns.

Apology

the throbbing shame
of all that I am not

and have not been;

the sorrow I have caused,

oblivious and knowing;

the taste of my failing
from infancy,
this human birth.

And drawing back
from this flavour,
watching the kindness
that lets shame
be just one spice
in a varied buffet

the love
that sets the table,
invitation to feast.

Olfactory assault,
would I even have been able
ever

to approach Mandela's cell?

Or stretch a hand,
crawling
in the jostling crowd,
dirt and turds,
to touch a saviour's stained cloak?

Or visited
the cold damp cave
of a starving monk
unwashed for years?

There is reverence
under my aversions,

nodding my nose,
deep prostrations

to the sweat and grime of it,

leaking and dripping,

embodied path.

Suck
on the gaiastream

o not to consume
only
but to live nourished

and nourishing

fill yourself
with the deep abundance
of sunlight

the endless rocking of waves
pull of the moon

juicy rain
plumping tectonic shifts
… this energy
not for taking

give it away freely

honouring you
in all that you perceive,

heal.

Ah Rumi
with your wineskins
and revelries

succulent woes and ecstasies

and me
like a nun called to dance
with the harlots

shedding my habit

finding the wink

our deserts
cold and hot
north and equator
then and a fleeting now

same sun.

Midwife of nowness
may I crouch
even bleary-eyed
exhausted

encourage push
and surrender

breathe deep

squint
at what I need to see

touching slippery unknowns
with tender welcome

summoning brave strength,

trusting I can catch

whatever comes.

Laughter in it,

how I tried to teach,
explaining life

and now
just open –

eyes and ears learning,
bouncing gently on each breath.

The questions everywhere,
unuttered,
my curiosity aroused
from the sleep of knowing

joy in my courage
to stand so unsure

inquisitive

each traveller a mystery.

Watch
for what loves you

and what makes you glad.

And when you feel
threat
to any of these

wash your hate

and all that fear

so a pliable smile

can tremble

on your moving skin.

I would show up now
if it weren't for all the tomorrows
cluttering my space

the questions
I feel burdened
to answer

his future
and hers

and planning
for opportunities

and stocking up
to be prepared.

The winnowing
we need to choose,
the winnowing
that forces
my surrender,

all these maybes
gripping;

may I thaw
now.

I sit
near this northern pole

(trying to acknowledge
how there is no north,

approaching the planet
from so many vectors)

and feel the stark rush
of April in Yukon.

How it looks barren
at first glance

and how many small slivers of green
are poking the surface

smaller than my fingernail,
like ten grains of sand
bathed in chlorophyll

and I take heart
in this natural miracle

our deep uprising.

I would write,
if I could,
about the caribou girls,

the ones in Sorels
who live with winter

and know the soft tickle
of sage still growing
under noses pressed to earth;

who feel vibration
from a thousand hooves
pounding ground

migration by tilt and sway,
axis dipping to sun.

It's quiet,
their kinship,
and can be blurred
by snowmobile
or harvest gun
or too much red wine
or deadlines

but they nod
unspoken greeting,
hitching longjohns,
deeply free.

www.ingramcontent.com/pod-product-compliance
Lightning Source LLC
Chambersburg PA
CBHW071926020426
42331CB00010B/2739